WOULD YOU RATHER...

BOOK FOR KIDS

EASTER EDITION

A Fun Easter Joke Book for
Kids, Boys, Girls, Teens and
The Whole Family

Jake Jokester

How to Play
~The Rules~

- You need at least 2 players to play.

- Choose who will go first. The first player chooses a question for the next player (player 2) to answer.

- Player 2 chooses one answer out of the 2 options

  You cannot answer "both" or neither".

  Optional rule: the answering player has to explain why they made the choice that they made.

- The player who answered the last question becomes the next asker. If there are more than 2 players, you can either pick any person to answer the next question or you can just ask the person next to you, going around in a circle.

Most important rule: Laugh, smile and have lots of fun!

Thanks for getting our book!

If you enjoy using it and it gives you lots of laughs and fun moments, we would appreciate your review on Amazon. Just head on over to this book's Amazon page and click "Write a customer review".

We read each and every one of them.

have a tree that grows jelly beans

or

have a tree that grows
chocolate eggs?

have a wooden egg

or

have a wooden tooth?

Would you rather...

collect bugs

or

collect eggs?

have wings like a bird

or

have feet like a rabbit?

have a candle in every color

or

have a flower in every color?

have bunny ears

or

have a bunny tail?

lose your marbles

or

lose your jelly beans?

pet a frog

or

pet a rock?

have a picnic with a teddy bear

or

have a conversation with a carrot?

play charades with your parents

or

read a fairytale with your grandparents?

have green grass for hair

or

have a plastic egg for the body?

bake Easter cookies

or

bake a birthday cake?

paint one hundred eggs

or

paint your whole house?

be responsible for a gigantic carrot

or

be responsible for a tiny chick?

Would you rather...

swim in a pool
full of melted chocolate

or

swim in a pool
full of caramel?

sneeze all Spring long

or

sleep all Spring long?

plant a tulip

or

plant a carrot?

sing on Easter Sunday

or

dance on Christmas day?

13

have White Rabbit from Alice in Wonderland as your friend

or

have Bugs Bunny from Looney Tunes as your friend?

look after rabbits

or

look after puppies?

have a striped pattern
on your Easter egg

or

have a circled pattern on
your Easter egg?

sleep on a bird's nest

or

sleep inside a pirate's chest?

Would you rather...

find a golden goose

or

find a magic tree?

be scratched by a cat

or

be kicked by a bunny?

collect flowers

or

collect chocolate eggs?

live in a giant rabbit hole

or

live in a cave in the forest?

wear a flower necklace

or

wear a flower crown?

eat a giant chocolate bunny

or

eat a giant jelly bean?

hard boil your eggs

or

soft boil your pasta?

go on an egg hunt

or

go for ice cream?

slide down a rainbow

or

dance in the rain?

walk on eggshells

or

walk on water?

decorate an Easter tree

or

play at a treehouse?

have a bunny-shaped cupcake

or

have a bunny-shaped pancake?

Would you rather...

work for the Easter Bunny

or

be one of Santa's elves?

receive a live chick
for Easter as a pet

or

receive a chocolate bunny
for Easter as a pet?

Would you rather...

have rain all Spring

 or

have snow all Summer?

wear a bunny costume

 or

wear a frog costume?

Would you rather...

have a fairy garden

 or

have a fairy godmother?

be allergic to chocolate

 or

be allergic to puppies?

play Easter bingo

or

make eggs from play-doh?

have grass for hair

or

have an Easter egg
for your nose?

go camping in the rain

or

sleep whilst the sun's out?

do a yard sale to earn money

or

do a lemonade stand
to earn money?

visit Easter Island

or

visit the hometown
of Santa Claus?

learn how to tie knots

or

learn how to tie a tie?

Would you rather...

win a bunny hop sack race

or

win a marshmallow eating contest?

be chased by the Easter bunny

or

be chased by the Tooth Fairy?

swim in confetti

or

dive in cake frosting?

build a castle out of egg cartons

or

build a castle out of seashells?

have a pet chicken

or

have a pet rabbit?

make fingerprint bunnies

or

make bunny-shaped cookies?

Would you rather...

go to church with your friends

or

go to a party with your parents?

make an Easter mask

or

watch an Easter movie?

egg your friend

or

egg your teacher?

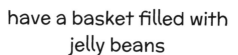

have a basket filled with
jelly beans

or

have a basket filled with
chocolate bunnies?

Would you rather...

find a ladybug

or

find a four-leaf clover?

spend a weekend at a farm

or

spend a weekend
at a chocolate factory?

Would you rather...

spend Easter abroad

or

spend Easter outdoors in nature?

spend Easter with
your best friend

or

spend Easter with the
Easter bunny?

live under a flower

 or

live under a mushroom?

go biking in the forest

 or

go swimming at the lake?

eat chocolate bunny filled
with mashed potatoes

or

eat chocolate bunny filled
with strawberry jam?

sing like a bird

or

hop like a bunny?

walk like a duck

or

look like a rabbit?

make a bird nest out of
your hat

or

make a bird nest out of
your shoe?

have a basket filled with toys

or

have a basket filled with treats?

receive an Easter basket

or

receive an Easter bonnet?

you could resurrect

 or

that you could walk on water?

sing an Easter song

 or

make an Easter postcard?

have hair as green as the grass

or

have hair as blue as the sky?

have chocolate arms

or

have chocolate legs?

make and eat boiled eggs

 or

make and eat an omelette?

have a golden egg

or

have a chocolate egg?

Would you rather...

spend a week in a teepee

 or

spend a night in a cave?

go swimming in the Spring

 or

go sunbathing in the Autumn?

Would you rather...

have a basket filled
with eggs

or

have a basket filled
with chicks?

tie a ribbon on a tree

or

tie your teacher's
shoelaces together?

Would you rather...

have jelly beans stuck on your teeth

or

wear a chocolate moustache?

have a jelly bean jar

or

have an Easter bunny basket?

do the chicken dance

or

do the bunny hop dance?

find melted candle wax in your hair

or

find melted candle wax on
your chocolate egg?

dance around the campfire

or

dance around a tree?

go to church on Easter

or

go to school on Easter?

discover a forest underwater

 or

discover a forest made
of chocolate?

have snow during Easter time

or

that it was warm during
Christmas time?

Would you rather...

have one big 2 meter high chocolate egg

or

have 80 small chocolate eggs?

go to an Easter parade

or

go to an Easter play in a theater?

Would you rather...

grow a plant

 or

grow a crystal?

go on an egg hunt

 or

go to the movies?

live inside an egg

or

live inside a cabbage?

have Easter brunch

or

go for an outdoor lunch
on Easter?

color a coloring book on Easter

 or

color an Easter egg on Easter?

watch a chick hatch

 or

watch a butterfly emerge
from its cocoon?

Would you rather...

have a lucky horseshoe

or

find a lucky four-leafed clover?

have rainbow-colored eyelashes

or

have butterfly wings for ears?

eat chicken eggs

or

eat quail eggs?

be a bunny for a day

or

be a squirrel for a day?

Would you rather...

have rainbow hair

 or

have sunflower nose?

skip April's Fool

or

skip Easter?

play 'capture the flag'

play 'tag, you're it!'?

have flowers for hair

have rain for eyelashes?

Would you rather...

have the wings of a chicken for arms

or

have the ears of a bunny?

forget to eat your Easter egg

or

forget the name of a friend?

eat a marshmallow bunny

 or

eat a candy egg?

ring the bells of Easter Sunday

 or

ring the bell for a school break?

Would you rather...

share your Easter candy

or

share your Halloween candy?

grow a magic carrot

or

grow a magic beanstalk?

lose your bike

or

lose your kite?

decorate 300 Easter bunny eggs

or

decorate 300 Easter bunny cookies?

Would you rather...

have a Spring break

 or

have an Autumn break?

be as curious as a kitten

 or

be as fluffy as a bunny?

go bird watching

or

go butterfly watching?

eat chocolate that tastes
like boiled eggs

or

eat boiled eggs that taste
like chocolate?

61

be as yellow as a chick

or

be as orange as a carrot?

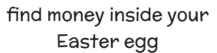

find money inside your
Easter egg

or

find a chick inside your
Easter egg?

paint a very heavy rock

or

paint a huge egg?

search for Easter eggs at the top of the mountain

or

search for Easter eggs under the ocean?

63

dress up as a bunny

or

dress up as a chicken?

have a water balloon fight
on Easter

or

have an egg fight on Easter?

find a robin's egg

or

find a dragon's egg?

wear an Easter bunny costume

or

wear a Santa Claus costume?

have an invisible egg

 or

have an egg that glows
in the dark?

hide Easter eggs

 or

find Easter eggs?

roll down a hill

or

climb a mountain?

swim in a pool of Easter punch

or

swim in a pool of Easter cocoa?

Would you rather...

fly a kite on Easter

or

go on a hike on Easter?

carry an uncooked egg

or

carry a huge Easter bunny egg?

egg your friend's house

or

egg your teacher's house?

make an Easter bonnet

or

make an Easter piñata?

Would you rather...

have bunny ears

or

have a bunny tail?

have a baby bunny as a pet

or

have a chick as a pet?

have a slice of carrot cake

or

have twelve Easter biscuits?

make friends with a talking fox

or

make friends with a talking rabbit?

Would you rather...

have an undercooked
egg for breakfast

or

have a 10 year old
egg for breakfast?

know the name of every flower

or

know the name of every star?

wear a bunny costume

or

wear a Mickey Mouse costume?

adopt a bunny

or

adopt a baboon?

Would you rather...

spend the night in the forest

or

spend the night at school?

have always Spring

or

have always Summer?

egg hunt

or

scavenger hunt?

ride a small horse

or

ride a giant hare?

Would you rather...

search for eggs with money inside

or

search for eggs with chocolate inside?

make your own Easter bread

or

make your own Easter wreath?

Would you rather...

eat carrots for a month

or

eat chocolate for a month?

paint an egg

or

paint a flower pot?

Would you rather...

wear clothes made of grass

or

wear clothes made of
bird feathers?

dig for worms

or

dig for gold?

have Easter lasted longer

or

that the summer came sooner?

read your book under a tree

or

make a book fort in
your living room?

play two truths and a lie on Easter

or

play hide and seek on Easter?

meet the Easter Bunny

or

meet a unicorn?

give all your bread to the ducks

or

give all your chocolate to your mom?

find a pot of gold at the
end of the rainbow

or

find a golden coin every day?

Would you rather...

eat a blue jelly bean that
tastes like vomit

or

eat a green jelly bean that
tastes like boogers?

have the most eggs

or

have the most friends?

Would you rather...

receive a really delicious Easter chocolate for a whole week

or

have no homework for a week?

be allergic to grass

or

be allergic to chocolate?

Would you rather...

hop like a bunny

or

slide around like a worm?

visit the zoo

or

play outdoors with
your friends?

Would you rather...

be a white bunny

or

be a black bunny?

read an Easter tale

or

travel back in time to
the first Easter

go horse riding

or

go flower picking?

have a lucky rabbit foot

or

meet Big Foot out in the forest?

go camping in the woods

or

go camping in your backyard?

feed the birds

or

feed the bunnies?

Would you rather...

have floppy ears

or

have droopy eyes?

that Easter Bunny didn't
bring any more eggs

or

that Santa didn't bring
any more gifts?

make a mud pie

 or

make a chocolate pie?

go to church every Sunday

 or

go to school every Sunday?

eat a real egg covered in chocolate

 or

eat a chocolate egg that's
covered in a real egg?

eat only carrots for a day

 or

eat only eggs for a week?

always walk around on all
fours (legs and arms)

 or

hop around like a rabbit?

meet the Easter bunny

 or

meet Santa Claus?

Would you rather...

grow beans on cotton balls

or

help eggs hatch?

follow some bunny footprints

or

follow an egg trail?

have new clothes for Easter

or

have a new haircut for Easter?

roll your eggs down the hill

or

have an egg roll?

steal honey from a bear

or

steal a carrot from
the Easter Bunny?

balance an egg on your nose

or

hang a spoon from your nose?

Would you rather...

have Easter every day

or

that it was Christmas only
once every four years?

have pink Easter eggs

or

have orange Easter eggs?

One last thing - we would love to hear
your feedback about this book!

If you found this activity book fun and useful, we
would be very grateful if you posted a short review on
Amazon! Your support does make a difference and we
read every review personally.

If you would like to leave a review, just head on
over to this book's Amazon page and click "Write a
customer review".

Thank you for your support!

Manufactured by Amazon.ca
Bolton, ON

18715375R00055